# The New 23 Laws of Power: a modern business take on Greene's 48 Laws

Maxim Moncalvo

# Contents

*Preface 6*

*Law 1: Never outshine the master 8*

*Law 2: Never put too much trust in friends, learn to use your enemies 11*

*Law 3: Conceal your intentions 14*

*Law 4: Always say less than necessary 17*

*Law 5: Make your reputation invulnerable 18*

*Law 6: Get others to do the work for you, but always take the credit 21*

*Law 7: Win through your actions, never through an argument 25*

*Law 8: Infection - avoid the unhappy and unlucky, rub shoulders with the successful 28*

*Law 9: Use selective honesty and generosity to disarm your victim 30*

*Law 10: When asking for help, appeal to people's self-interest, not mercy or gratitude 32*

*Law 11: Use absence to increase respect and honor 35*

*Law 12: Do not build fortresses to protect yourself: isolation is dangerous 38*

*Law 13: Do not commit to anyone 40*

*Law 14: Use the surrender tactic: transform weakness into power 42*

*Law 15: Recreate yourself 44*

*Law 16: Keep your hands clean 47*

*Law 17: Enter action with boldness 50*

*Law 18: Plan all the way to the end 53*

*Law 19: Make your accomplishments seem effortless 56*

*Law 20: Discover each man's thumbscrew 58*

*Law 21: Disdain things you can't have: ignoring them is the best revenge 62*

*Law 22: Despise the free lunch 64*

*Law 23: Preach the need for change, but never reform too much at once 67*

# Preface

The *48 Laws of Power* by R. Greene fundamentally shifted our way of approaching and dealing with power. The beauty of his work resides in the candid way he exposes embarrassing truths (*"everyone wants more [power]. In the world today, however, it is dangerous to seem too power hungry, [...] everything must appear civilized"*) and makes it clear how they apply to the majority of us. Power, he argues, is the most pursued goal in society, and those who know how to deal with it and accumulate more of it, are the ones who will come up on top. The *48 Laws of Power* is, then, an instruction manual on how to succeed in life.

The vast success of the book is proof that perhaps Greene does have a point, and that we might all be taking part in a ruthless game of power grab. We must recognize that many players are aware of this situation, and are equipped to play the game on a professional level.

If you haven't done so already, you now might be tempted to start looking for the *48 Laws of Power* on Amazon or at your local bookstore. The truth is, Greene's handbook was already outdated at the time he published it and is now more so. He relies on vibrant examples from the past, citing Chinese emperors and successful artists, French Kings, and con masters. Although these examples make for an interesting read, they are seldom applicable to the present, where power is much more subtle and decentralized. Moreover, many of the points he makes suffer from survivorship bias, as history tends to remember the grand and successful over the thousands who tried but failed miserably.

The potential behind the idea of the 48 Laws is, despite its flaws, undeniable. The book you are reading now, the New 23 Laws of Power is trying to unleash this potential in a modern business world made of complicated relationships, managers, CEOs, and business owners, rather than kings and emperors.

Another goal of this book is to democratize the application of these laws: not everyone is leading an army or dealing with the elite of the world. The New 23 Laws apply to those people who are in the process of climbing the ladder of power or want to consolidate their position in a competitive business environment.

You can apply the principles of this book to achieve a higher level of influence in both your work and personal life. But don't forget that you are not alone in playing this game: leverage this knowledge to become better at reading other players' power plays and avoid being subjugated.

# Law 1: Never outshine the master

Never attempt to look better than those above you in front of their peers or superiors. The temptation to outshine your superior could be strong, especially when you know the answer to a question better than they do. Outshining your superior is one of the biggest mistakes you can make: they may publicly thank you, but you are stirring up resentment, envy, and insecurity.

A bold intervention, especially if not supported by your superior, will make you seem overambitious, and people in power will think twice before allowing you in their circle, afraid that you will want to outshine them as well.

---

**Situation**

Your team manager has asked you to prepare some slides for the Business Review with the country's CFO. You put a lot of work into it and are finally satisfied with the result. You review your deck with your manager, and she is really impressed by the quality of your work.

You are invited to participate in the Business Review; although nothing is expected from you during the meeting, your boss is glad to give you some face-time with the CFO.

About half an hour into the meeting, the CFO asks

---

> about details on the pricing strategy of a competitor. Your boss struggles to answer and tries to steer the discussion in another direction, without much success. Even if the information is not part of the deck of slides, you know the answer, as you came across that piece of information just a couple of days before.
>
> *How do you intervene in this situation? Is directly replying to the CFO's request the best option? Were you to do so, how do you imagine your boss would react?*

Your role is not to know better than your superiors and show it off, but rather to advise them in the best possible way. In a situation of stall like the one described above, don't take over, but rather say something vague to guide them in the right direction.

Things change when you are meeting alone with your superior. In modern business, the master's power is not absolute like the one of a king. Leaders want smart people on their teams to leverage their talent and benefit from it. You must not be shy to demonstrate your skills to your superiors. Quite the opposite, let them reap the fruits of your talent and, in exchange, leverage them back as sponsors for your career. Any decent team leader knows that they can't maintain brilliant people close to themselves by hiding them from the external world, as they will inevitably escape the bounds of the master's control. Rather, the team leader will be happy to make good use of your work for as long as possible, before recommending you for a promotion and receiving praise for cultivating great talent.

Beware, though, not to assume that just because you get pampered during your alone time with your master, you can do anything you want. In Greene's words, *"entire books could be written about favorites who fell out of favor by taking their status for granted, for daring to outshine."*

# Law 2: Never put too much trust in friends, learn to use your enemies

Enemies are predictable and you naturally build defenses against them. Friends, on the other hand, can take you by surprise and know your weakest spots.

*"Men are more ready to repay an injury than a benefit, because gratitude is a burden and revenge a pleasure."*
Tacitus, c. A.D. 55-120

Expectations are key. A friend will expect a certain pattern of behaviors that you demonstrated in the past, perhaps during unprofessional situations. They expect to be treated well and as equals. Deviating from these behaviors will inevitably compromise your friendship and create tensions in your professional relationship. If you rebuke a friend for a job poorly done, they will be hurtful and resentful. Conversely, learn to work with your enemies and align their goals to yours for certain success (we will learn more in Law 10).

---
**Situation**

You are a project manager with two people on your team. The business is exploring options to expand in

---

> Eastern Europe, and you must advise the leadership team on which country to target first. You need your team members to provide you with a risks and opportunities report on the top three countries of the region.
>
> As the stakes are high, you are allowed to bring one extra person to your team. You decide to hire a long-time friend of yours, who is supposedly an expert in the field.
>
> One month later, you have your first checkpoint with the team: not only does this friend of yours not meet the deadline, but also the quality of his work is suboptimal and far behind his colleagues'. Worst of all, he seems unaware of his poor performance.
>
> *Are you able to maintain your friendship intact while giving him feedback on his poor performance? Wouldn't the situation be more comfortable if he wasn't a close friend of yours?*

The core problem is that in many friendships honesty steps aside to make space for politeness. You are going to compliment your friends on their intelligence, charm, and taste for the sake of being a good friend. They are not ready to receive honest and brutal feedback from you, as often is required in the workplace. Slowly, your former friends might start becoming enemies, as injuries are hidden but not forgotten, and accumulated over long periods. They will have plenty of time to plan behind your back and strike your weakest spot at the most convenient time.

Also, chances are that there is someone else outside your friend group that can help you achieve your goals better. To obtain power, you must ally with those who are able to further your interests in all situations. This might include putting adversities apart and allying with former enemies. Find those individuals with whom you can base a relationship on mutual self-interest, and you will uncover the quickest path to success.

# Law 3: Conceal your intentions

Keep people off-balance: seem familiar and predictable, then strike unexpectedly. Give no clue of your intentions, and feign interest in a red herring to lead their attention away from the objective. If you clearly show the path you intend to travel, anyone can build a palisade to prevent you from walking straight. But instead, if you point down different roads, your enemies will focus their efforts in occluding paths that you have no intention of walking, depleting their energies and giving you ample room to maneuver.

One powerful tool in throwing people off the scent is false sincerity. Openly express your belief in honesty and in talking straight, and follow it up with some apparent confession. We tend to like those who like us and open up with those who entrust us with their secrets (more on selective honesty in Law 9). Trade something of little relevance to you to get others to open up and implant the seeds of your deception.

### Situation
You are the head of e-commerce sales at a distributor of home appliances. The situation is very tense: last quarter's results just arrived, and they are worse than

anticipated. This is the culmination of a disastrous year, with sales across all three channels (e-commerce, retail chains, and specialized stores) dropping from the previous year. Your channel is the worst-performing, with total year sales decreasing double digits. Your superiors know that part of this is due to a new, bigger competitor entering the channel with stellar investments and that you have done your best to stem the loss with the available resources.

It's now time to budget for next year, and in a week's time you are required to share the expected sales results with your boss. You know she expects this negative trend to continue, so you already drafted your numbers to reflect this.

As you are heading out for lunch, the account manager of one of the biggest retailers asks if he can tag along with you. Lately, he's been meeting with you often, asking about details of your job and expressing his interest in e-commerce. As he's been in the role for more than two years, you start wondering whether he's planning a move to take your position.

As you return from lunch, you trash the next year's plan and start working on a new proposal, turning every stone to find opportunities for growth. After a week of long nights, you submit your revised numbers to your boss, assuring her that you are committing all of your efforts to reverse the negative trend.

> *By allowing others to see his goal, your colleague made it easier for you to build up defenses, entrenching your position against his attacks. What could he have done differently to catch you off balance?*

Another advantage of keeping those around you on their toes is the ability to hold the initiative on your side. As long as you retain the initiative, others will be forced to react to your moves, while you will be able to proactively plan what is coming next. As we'll discover in Law 18, planning all the way to the end provides you with an unquestionable competitive advantage.

## Law 4: Always say less than necessary

If you are the master of your thoughts, you'll be able to express them with a few, clear words. The more you say, the more likely you are to say something foolish. Once words are out, you cannot take them back.

*Down on his luck, [the screenwriter] Michael Arlen went to New York in 1944. To drown his sorrows he paid a visit to the famous restaurant "21." In the lobby, he ran into Sam Goldwyn, who offered the somewhat impractical advice that he should buy racehorses. At the bar Arlen met Louis B. Mayer, an old acquaintance, who asked him what were his plans for the future. "I was just talking to Sam Goldwyn ..." began Arlen. "How much did he offer you?" interrupted Mayer. "Not enough," he replied evasively. "Would you take fifteen thousand for thirty weeks?" asked Mayer. No hesitation this time. "Yes," said Arlen.*
   The Little, Brown Book of Anecdotes, C. Fadiman, 1985

Humans are creatures of imagination. We tend to wildly fantasize about what we don't know. Use this to your advantage: keep your words vague, and let others do the interpreting.

# Law 5: Make your reputation invulnerable

Battles can be won or lost before they even take place because of reputation.

The legend of general Chuko Liang takes place during China's War of the Three Kingdoms (A.D. 207 - 265). The general, also known as the "Sleeping Dragon", was reputed to be the most clever and crafty man in China. He was once resting in a small town with a handful of soldiers, after dispatching most of his men to a distant camp. Suddenly sentinels hurried in with the alarming news that an army led by his enemy Sima Yi was approaching. Outnumbered more than 1,000 to one, Chuko Liang's situation was hopeless. Without despair, he ordered his soldiers to open the city gates, sweep the ground and hide inside. He then took a seat on top of the city walls with his Guqin, a seven-string instrument, and started playing. Soon, the opposing army was standing in front of the open gates. At its head was Sima Yi, who instantly recognized the man on the wall as the Sleeping Dragon. As his soldiers itched to enter the unguarded town through its open gates, Sima Yi hesitated, held them back, and studied Liang on the wall. Then, he ordered an immediate and speedy retreat.

You can leverage your reputation to avoid battles that you are not ready to fight, but were your bluff to be called by your opponents, the damage caused could be irreversible. It takes years to build a reputation, but mere moments to destroy it.

In the beginning, you must work hard to establish a reputation for one outstanding quality. Aim for this quality to be the differentiating factor of your job. For example, if you work in the field of sales, build a reputation for being the most relentless salesperson. Make this known to as many people as possible, preferably through actions, and watch it spread like wildfire. You will notice that this single quality will instill respect from others, even if you lack many other qualities necessary to excel at your job. Whenever you provide unsatisfying results, your superiors will assume that you pushed your customers to the limit, and no one else could have done better. Sooner or later, you will take on different roles that require unrelated skills, but, as your reputation precedes you, much of the work is already done and you will command respect from the beginning.

> *"It is easier to cope with a bad conscience than with a bad reputation."*
>
> Friedrich Nietzsche, 1844 - 1900

By the same token, you can defeat your enemies by destroying their reputation, rather than winning on the field. A bad reputation stains everything around it and casts doubts on all the successes achieved in the past. Hollywood is swarming with examples of once crowd-favorite celebrities plummeting from grace because of scandals burning their reputation to the ground. An attack on reputation doesn't need to be necessarily true. Doubt is a powerful enough weapon. Cast doubts about someone's integrity, and let the rumors take them down. Leave the dirty job of spreading the word to the public: in case rumors are proven to be false, you don't want to stand out as the scandalmonger.

## Law 6: Get others to do the work for you, but always take the credit

Delegation and stealing are two faces of the same coin: leveraging the work and talent of others to further your own cause.

> *"Fools say that they learn by experience. I prefer to profit from others' experience."*
> Otto von Bismarck, 1815 - 1898

Be careful: sometimes you want to make it clear that your exceptional work was the result of your delegation skills. Hard work will get you only to a certain point in your career, after that, the ones who get on top are the ones who show better delegation and managerial skills. Micromanagement is the death of many careers, and yet it is so common. We tend to mistrust others and believe we can do everything better by ourselves, when in reality what is lacking is either our ability to choose the right people to do the job, or clear instructions on how to properly do it (i.e.: poor communication on our part). Sometimes, we tend to get lost in details whose finesse, according to ourselves, only we can perceive. What we don't realize is that those details are worthless in the bigger scheme of things. Often, the difference between "good enough" and "perfect" is not recognized and hence not worth spending time on.

Stealing, on the other hand, must be done gracefully. You don't have to hide the fact that you are stealing, but you must justify it by adding some value that the original owner of the work didn't possess.

> *"Everybody steals in commerce and industry.*
> *I've stolen a lot myself.*
> *But I know how to steal."*
> Thomas Edison, 1847 - 1931

---

**Situation**

Your boss assigns an urgent product research to you and your teammate Liam. You need to run surveys on a random sample of at least one hundred potential customers, analyze the results, and report on which product they liked best. From the beginning of the project, your partner is not much of a help: while you cut time out of your usual daily task and do most of the work, he keeps focusing on his routine tasks, putting the bare minimum effort into the new project. Towards the end of the assignment, you decide you had enough and confront him with the accusation of slacking off. To much of your surprise, Liam apologizes, and offers to take responsibility for the final part of interpreting the results and putting up a presentation for your superiors. You accept, but decide to keep a close eye on him and the final output, making sure no detail is left behind.

The presentation goes very well, and Liam mentions a couple of times during the talk how exceptional was your contribution. Your boss is so pleased that she decides to nominate this research for the "top 10" initiatives of the year across your company.

A month later, you receive a congratulatory email stating that your project made it to the final selection round of the awards and will be presented to the board in Chicago. You are delighted, but your enthusiasm fades when you notice that on the speaker's list only Liam's name appears. You ask your boss for an explanation, and she tells you that, as the budget is tight, they will be only flying him to Chicago. Meanwhile, vending-machine talk is all about "Liam's project" making it to the top.

*How do you react to such an injustice? Do you tell your boss about how little was his real contribution to the project? Sounding envious and a weak team player will just damage your own reputation. How could you have approached the situation differently?*

## Law 7: Win through your actions, never through an argument

In the realm of business and power, you must always think long-term. Any short-term satisfaction that you might get by "winning" an argument is often outweighed by the negative impression you give to the bystanders. Notice the quotation marks around the term winning. The reason is that often arguments aren't won, but rather parties just opt out by faking polite agreement. So you can never be sure about the outcome of your arguments, as you can't read other people's minds.

Winning through your actions is also one way to build your reputation. This law in action is demonstrated very well in the example starring Michelangelo in Greene's book:

*In 1502, in Florence, Italy, an enormous block of marble stood in the works department of the church of Santa Maria del Fiore. It had once been a magnificent piece of raw stone, but an unskillful sculptor had mistakenly bored a hole through it where there should have been a figure's legs, generally mutilating it. Piero Soderini, Florence's mayor, had contemplated trying to save the block by commissioning Leonardo da Vinci to work on it, or some other master, but had given up, since everyone* agreed that the stone had been ruined. So, despite the money that had been wasted on it, it gathered dust in the dark halls of the church.

This was where things stood until some Florentine friends of the great Michelangelo decided to write to the artist, then living in Rome. He alone, they said, could do something with the marble, which was still magnificent raw material. Michelangelo traveled to Florence, examined the stone, and came to the conclusion that he could in fact carve a fine figure from it, by adapting the pose to the way the rock had been mutilated. Soderini argued that this was a waste of time—nobody could salvage such a disaster—but he finally agreed to let the artist work on it. Michelangelo decided he would depict a young David, sling in hand.

Weeks later, as Michelangelo was putting the final touches on the statue, Soderini entered the studio. Fancying himself a bit of a connoisseur, he studied the huge work, and told Michelangelo that while he thought it was magnificent, the nose, he judged, was too big. Michelangelo realized that Soderini was standing in a place right under the giant figure and did not have the proper perspective. Without a word, he gestured for Soderini to follow him up the scaffolding. Reaching the nose, he picked up his chisel, as well as a bit of marble dust that lay on the planks. With Soderini just a few feet below him on the scaffolding, Michelangelo started to *tap lightly with the chisel, letting the bits of dust he had gathered in his hand to fall little by little. He actually did nothing to change the nose, but gave every appearance of working on it. After a few minutes of this charade he stood aside: "Look at it now." "I like it better," replied Soderini, "you've made it come alive."*

The 48 Laws of Power, Robert Greene, 1998

## Law 8: Infection - avoid the unhappy and unlucky, rub shoulders with the successful

Humans are extremely susceptible creatures. The people we surround ourselves with influence us in ways that go beyond our imagination. Just think that our close social relationships influence our microbiome composition (if you would like to know more about this fascinating subject, check the article *"Close social relationships correlate with human gut microbiota composition"* in Scientific Reports, by Dill-McFarland et al.)

The effect people around us have on our mind, behaviors and the image we project in the external world is even greater. You must learn to recognise infectious people, both in the negative and in the positive qualities. The former are usually those who approach their dissatisfaction with negativity. They will complain about everything and anything, blame others and never provide a solution for their own or others' problems. The shadows they cast obscure themselves and those around them. In defeat, they bring everyone down with them, in victory, they rise alone. The positive infectors, instead, deal with the same issues with the exact opposite approach: positivity. This does not mean that they are optimists, but rather that they either provide solutions or avoid complaining about their dissatisfactions. They shine light on the ones around them and create an environment where everyone feels naturally motivated and empowered to do better.

Learn to find the positive infectors that radiate those qualities that you lack. For example, if you are miserly, surround yourself with generous people, and you will feel inclined to follow their example.

*"Many things are said to be infectious. Sleepiness can be infectious, and yawning as well. In large-scale strategy when the enemy is agitated and shows an inclination to rush, do not mind in the least. Make a show of complete calmness, and the enemy will be taken by this and will become relaxed. You infect their spirit. You can infect them with a carefree, drunklike spirit, with boredom, or even weakness."*
A Book of Five Rings, M. Musashi, Seventeenth Century

# Law 9: Use selective honesty and generosity to disarm your victim

Give before you take. The giving softens the ground and makes it harder for the other person to notice the taking. It can take many different forms: a gift, a favor, or an "honest" admission. This form of manipulation is best employed in the first encounters with someone, as our first impressions last a long time. Sometimes a single gesture might not be enough, build on a series of acts and you will make yourself a reputation for honesty and generosity that will hardly be shaken.

Selective honesty is a falsely sincere admission that will be perceived by the counterpart as if we were opening and deeming them trustworthy. It's often enough to bring down the guard of the wariest people and have them reveal their own secrets to us. Selective kindness instead, in the form of a favor or a gift, is a calculated investment that will be repaid many times over, without the victim even acknowledging it. Consider these instruments as Trojan horses: seemingly innocuous devices able to effortlessly penetrate enemy lines.

Honesty and generosity are two powerful tools that you must learn to use not only to disarm but also to conceal your true intentions and build a reputation (Laws 3 and 5).

# Law 10: When asking for help, appeal to people's self-interest, not mercy or gratitude

Asking for help is a skill that involves understanding the person you are dealing with, and not confusing your needs with theirs. Mercy, if it exists, is a rare phenomenon and can be surely removed from the equation when talking about today's business environment. Gratitude, instead, is a heavy burden that many prefer to ignore rather than acknowledge and repay.

*In 433 B.C., just before the Peloponnesian War, the island of Corcyra (later called Corfu) and the Greek city-state of Corinth stood on the brink of conflict. Both parties sent ambassadors to Athens to try to win over the Athenians to their side. The stakes were high, since whoever had Athens on his side was sure to win. And whoever won the war would certainly give the defeated side no mercy. Corcyra spoke first. Its ambassador began by admitting that the island had never helped Athens before, and in fact had allied itself with Athens's enemies. There were no ties of friendship or gratitude between Corcyra and Athens. Yes, the ambassador admitted, he had come to Athens now out of fear and concern for Corcyra's safety.*

*The only thing he could offer was an alliance of mutual interests. Corcyra had a navy only surpassed in size and strength by Athens's own; an alliance between the two states would create a formidable force, one that could intimidate the rival state of Sparta. That, unfortunately, was all Corcyra had to offer.*

*The representative from Corinth then gave a brilliant, passionate speech, in sharp contrast to the dry, colorless approach of the Corcyran. He talked of everything Corinth had done for Athens in the past. He asked how it would look to Athens's other allies if the city put an agreement with a former enemy over one with a present friend, one that had served Athens's interest loyally: Perhaps those allies would break their agreements with Athens if they saw that their loyalty was not valued. He referred to Hellenic law, and the need to repay Corinth for all its good deeds. He finally went on to list the many services Corinth had performed for Athens, and the importance of showing gratitude to one's friends.*

*After the speech, the Athenians debated the issue in an assembly. In the second round, they voted overwhelmingly to ally with Corcyra and drop Corinth.*

The 48 Laws of Power, Robert Greene, 1998

Most people are pragmatic and locked inside needs of their own, no matter their wealth or social status. When applying for a favor, ask yourself "what would motivate this person to help me?". Try to find one side to solving your problem that would benefit them as well. And remember, gratitude is a worthless currency in both ways, you can't buy anything by promising your future gratitude, neither leveraging some sort of sense of obligation that the other party should feel for you. As shown in the example between Athens and Corinth, reminding the other party of past generosity with the expectation of being repaid will most likely cause irritation.

# Law 11: Use absence to increase respect and honor

The simple economic laws of supply and demand also apply to people's presence. Goods become more valuable when they are scarce. By the same token, you can increase the perceived value of your time by withdrawing your presence. For this to work, your value must be recognized and demanded in the first place, otherwise you only risk being forgotten.

> **Situation**
> You are a real estate manager finalizing the purchase of two apartments in the same complex from two different sellers. The apartments are identical, and the two sellers have been accommodating on the price, agreeing to close the sale at a 10% discount from the original listing price.
> The only difference was in the negotiation process: seller A was readily available to answer all of your questions and to meet with you in the apartment to discuss the details of the contract. Seller B, instead, had to reschedule multiple times and cut some meetings short, to the point that you felt exasperated and a bit anxious every time his name popped up in

the mail inbox. You heard from other real estate managers that this behavior was not uncommon for him. Nevertheless, everyone agreed that he is a fair businessman.

Both apartments are in good condition, but before renting them out you need to re-paint the walls and the doors. You estimate the refurbishing cost to be around 800 dollars each. You need to start renting them out in less than a month's time, at the start of peak tourist season. The average monthly rent is 2.000 dollars. A non-refurbished apartment could still be rented for a slightly lower price, but delaying the starting month would be a bad hit for the season.

Your remaining budget is 900 dollars, so you can afford to repaint one of the apartments. From your experience, you know that if you negotiate for the seller to pay for the painting job you have a 40% chance of success, a 40% chance that they say no, and a 20% chance to delay the sale.

*Given the past experience with the sellers, which one would you ask? Knowing that the selling price and conditions are the same, do you feel one seller holds more power than the other? Imagine selling one hundred apartments instead of one: the economic*

> *effect of the seller's power would be material.*

Think about the extreme example of withdrawal: someone's death. An artist's valuation of their work tends to be greater after their death, it becomes surrounded by an aura of respect and mystery. In simpler terms, think about your own reaction when someone struggles to show up because of their filled agenda and has to plan time in advance. They demand much more respect than someone who's readily available at any time because we assume their day is full of important events that have priority over us.

## Law 12: Do not build fortresses to protect yourself: isolation is dangerous

Isolating in a fortress might seem like the safest defense against your enemies, instead, it makes for an easy target, far from useful information and the help of allies. The isolated will lose access to the sources of their power, while someone else will find a way to tap into those same resources behind their back.
Influence and power are human creations that can only be maintained by exercising them regularly. Isolation takes this practice away. If you exercise your power exclusively through a proxy, you will eventually shift your own power to the proxy itself.

Do not confuse isolation and carefully planned absence (Law 11). Absence is a power-building tool that you must hone by regularly reappearing at your will. In absence, others crave your company but don't have access to it. In isolation, everyone knows where you are, but don't have an incentive to be in your company.

The new era of working from home and videoconferences is a dangerous one when it comes to isolation. Productivity is high, mostly because we tend to revolve our professional relationships exclusively around work-related tasks. We dedicate much less time to informal talk and we know less and less about the people who move around us. As the breadth of relationships is narrowing, we lose access to powerful information that was transmitted through word of mouth. Avoid making your talks all about transactional matters. Those able to maintain an influence network under these conditions will be the ones having a competitive advantage in growing their careers.

## Law 13: Do not commit to anyone

Avoid taking sides, especially when it's not your own battle. Instead, maintain your independence and try to play the referee. Let them pursue you by giving them hope but never satisfaction.

We naturally tend to take sides when asked, because we don't want to let people down. We think they'll be angry and disappointed, but the reality is that often refusals provoke not anger but a kind of respect. You make yourself ungraspable rather than succumbing. As your reputation for independence grows, so does the desire of others. Who will be the lucky one to get you to commit? And desire spreads like a virus: we tend to find more desirable people who are desired by many others.

*The kites and the crows made an agreement among themselves that they should go halves in everything obtained in the forest. One day they saw a fox that had been wounded by hunters lying helpless under a tree, and gathered round it. The crows said, "We will take the upper half of the fox." "Then we will take the lower half," said the kites. The fox laughed at this, and said, "I always thought the kites were superior in creation to the crows; as such they must get the upper half of my body, of which my head, with the brain and other delicate things in it, forms a portion." "Oh, yes, that is right," said the kites, "we will have that part of the fox." "Not at all," said the crows, "we must have it, as already agreed." Then a war arose between the rival parties, and a great many fell on both sides, and the remaining few escaped with difficulty. The fox continued there for some days, leisurely feeding on the dead kites and crows, and then left the place hale and hearty, observing, "The weak benefit by the quarrels of the mighty".*

Indian Fables

You can take your strategy one step further by stirring up quarrels and offering to mediate, instead of waiting for dissension to come up itself. Once the fighting is over, the loot will be ready to be picked up by whoever has the most energy left.

The masters of this strategy do not completely stand aside, as that could be perceived as offensive. Instead, they show interest in the struggle and pretend to be looking for a solution. Outwards, they seem caring and interested, but inwards, they do not let external problems eat away their energy. Don't succumb to the emotions of others' battles or your time will be wasted solving their worries.

## Law 14: Use the surrender tactic: transform weakness into power

When you cannot win, surrender to give yourself time to recover and plan a different path to victory. Often, the winning side forgets too quickly about those who surrender, thinking them weak and submissive, and shifts attention to other fronts, gradually weakening the grip on the surrendered party. Power comes and goes, sometimes unexpectedly. You can have your chance of triumph only if you are around to grab it.

Sometimes, you want to surrender even before losing. Overreactions are often what get us in trouble. Violent, strong actions often open up a vicious cycle of reactions that ultimately leaves us in ruins. When provoked, respond blandly by bowing your head and you will make a fool of those taunting you. Weak or no reaction at all is demotivating to the attacker.

*Voltaire was living in exile in London at a time when anti-French sentiment was at its highest. One day walking through the streets he found himself surrounded by an angry crowd. "Hang him. Hang the Frenchman," they yelled. Voltaire calmly addressed the mob with the following words: "Men of England' You wish to kill me*

*because I am a Frenchman. Am I not punished enough for not being born an Englishman?"*
*The crowd cheered his thoughtful words, and escorted him safely back to his lodgings.*
  The Little, Brown Book of Anecdotes, C. Fadiman, 1985

When you find yourself in the position of the victor, remember this law, and make sure not to be fooled by the surrender tactic. Go the extra mile not to leave any hope for your opponent, or you might regret it in the future.

Often, it's just not possible to crush our enemies totally. Businesses are regulated and enemies cannot be sent to exile. In these cases, the best option is to influence their future development to make sure they don't interfere. For example, if you fought for and won a promotion over someone else who might plot against you, you can try to sponsor them for a promotion in a division far away from yours.

## Law 15: Recreate yourself

Be the master of your role instead of letting others define it for you. Pre-assigned roles come with an allotted amount of power. By accepting your role, you limit your power to that defined amount. Recreate yourself and your role to escape the defined boundaries: not only will you be walking a path with a potentially unlimited amount of power, but also you will make a reputation for being able to go above and beyond mere job descriptions.

No one is naturally fit for multiple roles: we need training and time on the job before excelling in different fields. This is why in order to recreate yourself you must first of all be a good actor. Create a new identity and obtain a new role first, then learn and excel at it.

The first step in shaping your new image is self-consciousness. You must be aware of yourself, your appearance, your skills, and your weaknesses. You also need to understand what image others have of you. Often, you will find that your reputation is much more polarized around a certain skill than you imagined. Don't be surprised or let down: while you see yourself every day and know what you are capable of, others see you mostly in your role, which may be repetitive or limited in breadth. This is your starting point: understand what areas you must underscore to construct the image you want of yourself and follow with the suitable behavior. Sometimes, your act must be theatrical, to wipe away any remaining stain of a role you don't want to be associated with.

> *"Learn to play many roles, to be whatever the moment requires. Adapt your mask to the situation—be protean in the faces you wear."*
> The 48 Laws of Power, Robert Greene, 1998

A perfect opportunity for recreating yourself is when you join a new company. Take the time to carefully plan the first impression you want to make on your new coworkers. Think about how you want to shape the new role, what you want to be renowned for, how you want to build your career path, and what skills are required to follow that path. Write down your answers to some of the frequently asked questions to new joiners (For example: why did you leave your previous company? What is the first impression of the new role? What is important to you for your success? What kind of people do you like working with?).

In the first few months in a new role, nobody is expecting much from you. This is the opportunity to work on your image, exaggerate some behaviors if you know you naturally tend to suffer in those areas (for example, try to talk to as many people as possible both during working hours and outside of them if you know you are naturally shy and tend to isolate yourself). Make a reputation for yourself in those areas you want to stand out and collect the dividends for years to come.

## Law 16: Keep your hands clean

Protect your reputation by avoiding blame for unpleasant news and dreadful actions. Have scapegoats ready to take the fall: our appearances often depend more on what we conceal rather than on what we reveal. It's normal to make mistakes along the way, but excuses and apologies are often not enough. Avoid the blame altogether and you will spare yourself a lot of work trying to regain trust.

Sometimes, you will find yourself planning something necessary but ugly, or you will be in a position of delivering bad news to your superiors. In these cases, try to use a *cat's paw* - someone unrelated to yourself - to carry the deed or deliver the news. Be the bearer of cheerful and bright messages, and people will associate you with those positive feelings.

---

**Situation**

Remember the situation analyzed in Law 1, where your boss is having a hard time replying to the CFO's questions while presenting a deck that you prepared for her. Given the teaching of that law, it would be unwise to step up and outshine your superior showing that you possess information that she doesn't.

In this circumstance, you have the opportunity to

> exploit Law 16 but, rather than doing it for yourself, you would do that to protect your boss: step up by acknowledging that the missing information is your fault, that you provided it in an unclear and confusing manner and that you apologize. Then, either reply to the question directly, or heavily hint in the right direction for your boss to pick up and provide the right answer.
>
> By acknowledging your mistake in this situation, you are killing two birds with one stone: your boss will be grateful for getting her out of trouble, and the CFO will be impressed by your candor and confidence.
>
> *What would be the CFO's reaction if, instead of admitting the mistake yourself, your boss pointed out that the lack of information was your fault? If you were in her shoes, would you have exploited the scapegoat in this situation?*

As outlined in the Situation box, this Law is really context-dependent. Blaming someone else becomes a sign of weakness and lack of control if the fault, or at least part of it, can be evidently traced back to you. Even worse is blaming someone on your team, one of your employees, or anyone under your management's influence. This clearly shows a lack of control and delegation skills.

Sometimes, especially at the beginning of your career, you will not be in a position to use scapegoats to cover your mistakes or cat's paws to do whatever you don't want to be seen doing. In this case, you should not try to hide behind weak excuses, but rather be confident, bold, and admit your mistakes. Show growth by avoiding the same errors twice, rather than trying to appear untainted in the first place.

Occasionally, you will want to offer yourself as a scapegoat or as a bearer of bad news. Again, this is relevant in the first phases of your career, where pleasing some of your direct superiors is more important than keeping a spotless reputation. Whenever you feel like blame will be placed upon you, try to offer yourself proactively to impress your superiors. Make this a virtue and not a habit: if you offer yourself too often you will be considered as nothing else but an instrument to shift the blame, and the damages to your reputation might be unrepairable.

## Law 17: Enter action with boldness

There is no example I can think of where an action taken with a timid approach has resulted in a better outcome than the same action taken with boldness. Being bold and confident irradiates positivity and conviction to those surrounding us (see Law 8 for the power of infection). By the same token, our execution will be impacted negatively by our doubts and hesitations: better not to attempt something we are unsure of.

Imagine competing *against* someone bold versus someone hesitant. I guarantee in the first case you will feel much more in danger than the latter. Unless your goal is to distract your opponent by faking hesitation and then striking boldly and unexpectedly (Law 3), your mere negative approach to a situation will infect all players and outcomes.

Boldness and audacity can also work as a signaling mechanism, for example when negotiating your salary. The hiring party has limited information on your worth, and pricing is a key element. Ask for a low salary, and all your efforts will be tainted by an air of mediocrity. Yes, your CV is impressive and the interviews went well, but perhaps you lack leadership skills. Shoot for the stars instead, and everything you do will be perceived as excellent. Do you only have two years of experience in the role? It must have been a quick learning curve packed with responsibilities.

In a group setting, the most hesitant ones are the ones who fail first. The most ordinary and boring tasks will be pushed onto them, and as soon as the opportunity presents itself, they will be used as scapegoats by the entire group. The daring inspire fear and people will think twice before confronting them, while the fearful are marking themselves as easy targets.

It's important not to confuse the bold with the extrovert and the timid with the introvert: those are two different sets of attributes that are not related to each other. The extrovert who loves to talk much and talk loud might lack the few cunning words that cut through the opponent's armor at the right time: a single arrow to the joints rather than a full quiver on a wooden shield.

*"Always set to work without misgivings on the score of imprudence. Fear of failure in the mind of a performer is, for an onlooker, already evidence of failure...*
*Actions are dangerous when there is doubt as to their wisdom; it would be safer to do nothing."*
Baltasar Grácian, 1601-1658

Humans are timid by nature. We are programmed to be lazy and avoid energy-expensive situations, such as strong confrontation or anything that goes beyond our normal routine. In our minds, we tend to exaggerate the negative consequences of our actions, especially when we believe they will upset someone else. When taking action, invest that extra energy necessary to be bold and fearless and it will pay off by eliminating obstacles in your future course.

# Law 18: Plan all the way to the end

Only the fool can enter action with boldness not having planned all the way to the end. The temptation to improvise and adapt *en course* might be strong, but the results are rarely as good as when a defined plan is followed from the beginning. Think about the stock market: 92% of actively managed funds underperformed the S&P 500 (passive index investment) over the last 15 years.

When you have planned your moves ahead, temptation and emotions become manageable, as you can rely on your longer-term plan whenever encountering a bumpy road. Many times, the main reason for failure is anxiety driven by uncertainty. A defined plan with the ending clearly in view will remove this uncertainty.

*In ancient times a king of Tartary was out walking with some of his noblemen. At the roadside was an Abdal, who cried out: "Whoever will give me a hundred dinars, I will give him some good advice." The king stopped, and said: "Abdal, what is this good advice for a hundred dinars?" "Sir," answered Abdal, "order the sum to be given to me, and I will tell it to you immediately." The king did so, expecting to hear something extraordinary. The dervish said to him: "My advice is this: Never begin anything until you have reflected what will be the end of* it." At this the nobles and everyone else present laughed, saying that the Abdal had been wise to ask for his money in advance. But the king said: "You have no reason to laugh at the good advice this abdal has given me. No one is unaware of the fact that we should think well before doing anything. But we are daily guilty of not remembering, and the consequences are evil. I very much value this dervish's advice."

The king decided to bear the advice always in his mind, and commanded it to be written in gold on the walls and even engraved on his silver plate.

Not long afterward a plotter desired to kill the king. He bribed the royal surgeon with a promise of the prime ministership if he thrust a poisoned lancet into the king's arm. When the time came to let some of the king's blood, a silver basin was placed to catch the blood. Suddenly the surgeon became aware of the words engraved upon it: "Never begin anything until you have reflected what will be the end of it." It was only then that he realized that if the plotter became king he could have the surgeon killed instantly, and would not need to fulfill his bargain. The king, seeing that the surgeon was now trembling, asked him what was wrong with hun. And so he confessed the truth, at that very moment. The plotter was seized; and the king sent for all the people who had *been present when the abdal gave his advice, and said to them: "Do you still laugh at the dervish?"*

Caravan of Dreams, Idries Shah, 1968

Your actions must end when the goal is met. Don't overextend your success without revising your plan, or you risk jeopardizing all the good you obtained so far.

Of course, plans can fail. Alternative routes must be built into your plan, and also a viable fallback strategy must be in place in case the end goal is no longer attainable. Improvising during a crisis might keep you afloat until you encounter the next crisis. Instead, fallback plans make sure that your retreat is well protected and give you the necessary time to recover.

# Law 19: Make your accomplishments seem effortless

You must continually practice and refine your public appearances but display nonchalance and grace to appear more powerful. Never expose the sweat and labor behind your work, or you'll appear weak and not worthy of greater responsibilities.

Some think that complaining about the time and effort they put in their work attracts sympathy and respect for their diligence and commitment. This might be true, but it's usually limited to those coworkers who are not above your level and, in turn, like to revolve their conversations around whining about how hard life is. As we have seen in Law 8 (Infection: Avoid the Unhappy and Unlucky), you should steer clear of such companies.

Processes and techniques can be copied, however complex they are, talent and genius are natural traits that few possess: build a reputation for the latter and people will admire and even fear you. It will appear as if your power is much greater than what you are showing.

Properly applying this law means that, as a matter of fact, you will need to put even more effort into your work, as the output needs to be adorned by a flawless delivery. You need to prepare the setting and plan the execution in detail.

Be careful with your subordinates: they will follow your example, so you must not confuse making accomplishments seem effortless with just working fewer hours. On the opposite, you want to set an example for commitment and devotion.

## Law 20: Discover each man's thumbscrew

The most straightforward form of power is control over other people's actions. It can be direct, in the form of hierarchies and orders, or indirect in the form of influence. The most powerful influencing tool is playing on others' weaknesses. Everyone has a weakness, an insecurity, an uncontrollable need, or a secret pleasure. Find it and leverage it to your advantage.

Information plays a key role in this Law. You need to know as much as possible about your target: everyday conversations and social encounters are the richest mines of weaknesses. Be a good listener and use selective honesty (Law 9) to make others open to you, then gather all the information you need. Often, you will find that someone's weakness is the opposite of a trait they overtly show in everyday's work. The ones who make a show of confidence might be motivated by covering up an insecurity.

Insecurity and unhappiness are the two most common emotional voids. The former makes people seek any kind of social validation: compliment and make them feel better about their social standing, and they will constantly come back to you. The unhappy are willing to go any length to fill this void, but usually it doesn't last very much. They come back for a dose of happiness and they slowly become addicted. Be the source of their happiness and they will do anything for you.

When gathering information, it's important not to be too obvious: keep your intentions concealed. If your target sees through the show of selective honesty and intimacy you will achieve the opposite of what you set up for: your actions and questions will reveal everything about you and your intentions. There are many different reactions to discovering that one is being tricked: someone tends to forget it and carry on with their lives, others will seek revenge, going further than you could imagine.

*In the late 1910s some of the best swindlers in America formed a con-artist ring based in Denver, Colorado. In the winter months they would spread across the southern states, plying their trade.*
*In 1920 Joe Furey, a leader of the ring, was working his way through Texas, making hundreds of thousands of dollars with classic con games. In Fort Worth, he met a sucker named J. Frank Norfleet, a cattleman who owned a large ranch. Norfleet fell for the con. Convinced of the riches to come, he emptied his bank account of $45,000 and handed it over to Furey and his confederates. A few days later they gave him his "millions," which turned out*

to be a few good dollars wrapped around a packet of newspaper clippings.

Furey and his men had worked such cons a hundred times before, and the sucker was usually so embarrassed by his gullibility that he quietly learned his lesson and accepted the loss. But Norfleet was not like other suckers. He went to the police, who told him there was little they could do. "Then I'll go after those people myself," Norfleet told the detectives. "I'll get them, too, if it takes the rest of my life." His wife took over the ranch as Norfleet scoured the country, looking for others who had been fleeced in the same game. One such sucker came forward, and the two men identified one of the con artists in San Francisco, and managed to get him locked up. The man committed suicide rather than face a long term in prison.

Norfleet kept going. He tracked down another of the con artists in Montana, roped him like a calf, and dragged him through the muddy streets to the town jail. He traveled not only across the country but to England, Canada, and Mexico in search of Joe Furey, and also of Furey's right-hand man, W. B. Spencer. Finding Spencer in Montreal, Norfleet chased him through the streets. Spencer escaped but the rancher stayed on his trail and caught up with him in Salt Lake City. Preferring the mercy of the law to Norfleet's wrath, Spencer turned himself in. Norfleet found Furey in Jacksonville, Florida, and *personally hauled him off to face justice in Texas. But he wouldn't stop there: He continued on to Denver, determined to break up the entire ring. Spending not only large sums of money but another year of his life in the pursuit, he managed to put all of the con ring's leaders behind bars. Even some he didn't catch had grown so terrified of him that they too turned themselves in. After five years of hunting, Norfleet had single-handedly destroyed the country's largest confederation of con artists. The effort bankrupted him and ruined his marriage, but he died a satisfied man.*

The 48 Laws of Power, Robert Greene, 1998

## Law 21: Disdain things you can't have: ignoring them is the best revenge

We are surrounded by an infinite number of events, things, and people but we can process only a very limited number of them. We choose what enters our attention span and what is left out. Acknowledging petty problems rather than focusing on constructive activities is a decision that we make.

As we are naturally loss-averse, we tend to overemphasize what we don't or can't have: we give credibility to small worries and we make them worse and more visible by struggling to fix them. Learn to shift your attention away from those issues you have no control over, and channel your energies wherever you can influence the outcomes. If you are overwhelmed by a myriad of problems that fog your judgment, try guided meditation: a clear head is the first step in the right direction.

Seeming unaffected by minor events is also a matter of image: nobody wants a leader who panics at the hint of the slightest headwind. You must stand erect and not let the irritating matters drag you down. By doing so, you will radiate an air of security and confidence that will elevate you above the rest.

Sometimes, petty problems or irritating opponents need to be taken care of. The best strategy, in this case, is to do away with them in the most discreet way. It could be expensive, but it avoids inflating those issues by drawing attention to them (just look up how Airbnb manages potential PR crises).

*A monkey was carrying two handfuls of peas. One little pea dropped out. He tried to pick it up, and spilled twenty. He tried to pick up the twenty, and spilled them all. Then he lost his temper, scattered the peas in all directions, and ran away.*

Fables, Leo Tolstoy, 1828-1910

## Law 22: Despise the free lunch

*"Remember: Free is a price. It's a price that disproportionately grabs our attention."*
Dollars and Sense, Dan Ariely and Jeff Kreisler, 2017

Usually, we pay money for goods and services. That is why when we think about *free*, we assume it's without a monetary charge. What we don't account for is that whatever we are accepting for *free*, comes with obligations. When we pay the full price, we are free from obligation and gratitude, when we don't pay, we are not. If you are enjoying something for *free* without the feeling of obligation, then it's likely that you are the product (e.g.: online advertising).

Understand that everything has a cost: it might be money, time, gratitude, or peace of mind. How much time do we waste comparing prices at a supermarket, often to save just some change, and reducing our enjoyment of the product later? How often do we choose the cheapest option when renovating our house, and then have to redo everything a second time, as we can't stand looking at how poorly the walls were painted?

*Akimoto Suzutomo, a wealthy adherent of the tea ceremony, once gave his page 100 Ryo (gold pieces) and instructed him to purchase a tea bowl offered by a particular dealer. When the page saw the bowl, he doubted it was worth that much, and after much bargaining got the price reduced to 95 Ryo. Days later, after Suzutomo had put the bowl to use, the page proudly told him what he had done. "What an ignoramus you are!" replied Suzutomo. "A tea bowl that anyone asks 100 pieces of gold for can only be a family heirloom, and a thing like that is only sold when the family is pressed for money. And in that case they will be hoping to find someone who will give even 150 pieces for it. So what sort of fellow is it who does not consider their feelings? Quite apart from that, a curio that you give 100 Ryo for is something worth having, but one that has only cost 95 gives a mean impression. So never let me see that tea bowl again!" And he had the bowl locked away, and never took it out.*

The 48 Laws of Power, Robert Greene, 1998

If you are about to take something or ask for help, it's a good strategy to give before you take. An unexpected gift will soften up your targets and put them under obligation when you are ready to make your requests. Don't fall for it when others try to use this strategy on you: train yourself to take decisions ignoring the burden of gratitude, or giving it the rightful weight.

> *"Money is never spent to so much advantage as when you have been cheated out of it; for at one stroke you have purchased prudence."*
> Arthur Schopenhauer, 1788-1860

## Law 23: Preach the need for change, but never reform too much at once

Organizations need to constantly change to keep up with the market. Senior executives will promote a certain degree of progress to keep up with the times, and reorganize people and hierarchies accordingly. Often, highly salaried employees are hired because of their role in changing the ways of working and the culture of a workplace. But don't get confused: voicing for too much change is not appreciated. Progress must be gradual and at the level decided by executives. Everyone in the organization agrees that some transformation is needed, and the right amount is the one dictated by upper management, no more, no less.

Be at the forefront of change, and adopt new behaviors as advertised by your leaders, but don't make a show of unconventional ideas and drastic changes. You might have the right plans, but flaunting them will make it seem like you are seeking attention and looking down on the well-established culture. Share your original proposals with a selected group, and do so gradually, making sure you are not overthrowing the basis of their power.

The reason you don't want to be seen as a revolutionist is that most people won't change their thinking habits, even when presented with sound logical arguments. Politics and investment are the two fields where we see this phenomenon most clearly: once someone picks their flag, they will only seek and accept information that confirms their belief and refuse and ignore information that goes against them (confirmation bias).

Sometimes, ideas might involve people losing their job or their power. In these cases, discussions will be much more heated and might lead to the creation of factions. Usually, the prevailing faction is the one rooting for the status quo, but it might not be the one that plays in your favor. One trick is to seem to disagree with the dangerous ideas, but giving them exposure in doing so. You might go as far as suggesting faulty arguments for defending the status quo, making sure to use a *cat's paw* to expose them to the public (remember Law 16).

> **Situation**
> Chyou was just hired by the White Power Tools Corp. to lead the international pricing division. Having worked in a leading FMCG company for the last five years, she is considered an expert in this area. On the contrary, the White Power Tools Corp. never invested

much in its pricing division and is now lagging behind competitors. To regain their position as leaders of the industry, executives laid out a change plan for the next three years, and chose Chyou to lead the efforts.

Chyou is a very motivated young manager: whatever she lacks in experience, she makes up for with willpower and dedication. She is determined to improve the situation at her new company and show off her talents to win a quick promotion.

What she wasn't expecting is how poor the situation in her division is: systems are outdated, teams are short-staffed and employees have been working for decades on the same routines. Moreover, from her point of view, the plan laid out by upper management lacks ambition and won't fix the situation.

*"In my old company, we used better systems"*, *"in my old company, your job was done by a machine"*, *"in my old company, we used forecasting models"*, *"in my old company..."*. Soon, people started wondering what is she even doing here if she liked her *"old company"* so much. Her team has been working overtime most days because, on top of the three-year change plan, Chyou set more ambitious targets to be reached sooner.

In just a couple of months, people started resenting her and the change she stood for. They would get in her way for the sake of doing so, jeopardizing not only her more ambitious plan but also the original strategy laid out by the executive team.

*It is one thing to have the right ideas to lead your company to success, it is quite another to implement them. People are reluctant to change, especially if:*
*1) there is no payoff for them;*
*2) they need to get out of their comfort zone;*
*3) they have not changed in many years;*
*4) they don't believe in the people leading the change.*

*Chyou could have conformed to the original plan, successfully achieving the (easy) goals set by the executive management, thereby gaining the trust of both her superiors and her team. Then, she could have planted the seed for a more radical change with much more ease.*

www.ingramcontent.com/pod-product-compliance
Lightning Source LLC
Chambersburg PA
CBHW070120230526
45472CB00004B/1347